TO WORSHIP IN
STILLNESS

TO WORSHIP IN STILLNESS

Thirty Reflective Services
by

SUSAN SAYERS

Kevin Mayhew

First published in 1991 by
KEVIN MAYHEW LTD
Rattlesden
Bury St Edmunds
Suffolk IP30 0SZ

ISBN 0 86209 162 4

Front cover: Lippi, Angel Adoring.
Reproduced by courtesy of the Trustees,
The National Gallery, London.

Cover designed by Graham Johnstone
Typesetting and page creation by Anne Hallam
Printed in Hong Kong by Colorcraft Limited

CONTENTS

Introduction

To Worship in Stillness aims to provide a resource
for parishes and ecumenical groups who want to
have shared worship involving stillness, silence,
music and reflection. The book contains 30 forms
of worship, which nurture a deeper sense of
wonder and adoration through enjoying the
company of the Lord, and reflecting on many
different facets of the nature of God.

Each reflection focuses on a particular quality in
the God we worship, such as wisdom, compassion
or refreshment. Naturally the forms of worship
vary considerably according to the theme, but all
provide times of extended silence, scripture
reading, and spoken exchanges between leaders
and everyone else. Suitable chants, hymns and
choruses are suggested, all of which are included
in the book, after the forms of worship.

Many people are unused to silence, and need
encouragement and help in settling to stillness
and using it profitably. So for each time of silence
I have included written but unspoken direction.
The length of silences can obviously be varied to
suit the group and the occasion, but I feel that
anything less than two minutes is really only a
pause, and would not allow people sufficient time
to get down into the silence and gain from it.

I have also suggested that there should be no
exact beginning to the worship. So as to feel part
of the constant wave of praise which continues all
over the world as our planet turns, begin the
singing with a small group before people start
arriving. Then, as they come, there is no sense of
waiting for a performance to start, but rather a
sense of being drawn into the climate of worship
which spans time and eternity.

If you are a small group in a large building,
arrange a small area within it for everyone to be
gathered, so as to emphasise that this is corporate
worship – the body of Christ's people together.
Think also about the most suitable way to arrange
seating; a semi-circle or square with space in the

centre may be more helpful than long straight rows. Or, during good weather, you may like to try gathering somewhere outside. The singing is an important part of the worship. Although it is lovely to have instrumental accompaniment, this is certainly not essential, so don't be deterred from singing because you have no accompanist available. Have one or two people to lead everyone in, and you may well find that the singing takes on new life.

It is often helpful to have flowers, foliage, candles, a picture, or some other focal point for people to use. This should always be arranged simply and prayerfully, and well in advance, so that there are no last-minute preparations going on when people start arriving. We need to create an atmosphere which is conducive to wholehearted worship and receptivity to God. To him be the glory.

God of Peace

As people are gathering to worship, sing *Nada te turbe* **(39)**, continuing until everyone is still and relaxed. Then let the singing get quieter and quieter, so as to take you all down into God's stillness.

Silence During this time, breathe OUT the day's worries and pressure; breathe IN the peace of eternal God.

Leader 'Peace I give you,
my peace I give to you,' says the Lord.

All Lord, give us your peace; *(pause)*
help us to accept the peace you give.
May your peace soak up our thoughts,
flood our feelings,
still our bodies,
fill this place.
In your peace let us relax, now,
accepting ourselves and each other
as you are accepting us.
Lord, give us your peace.

Silence Think over the words you have just said, and allow God's peace to soak into you.

Sing *Peace, perfect peace* **(47)** v.1.
Sing it through two or three times.

Leader Listen to these words of Jesus
and let them take root in you.

Reading Mark 4.35-41

Leader This is the word of the Lord
All Thanks be to God.

Silence/Music
Music suggestions: Mozart, *Piano Concerto no.23 (Slow movement)*; Fauré, *Pavane*.
While you listen, think over the words you have heard. Allow God to speak to your need for peace in the storms and worries of your own life.

Allow him to take control over them and bring
his calm into all areas of your life. If you wish,
have music continuing very softly while you pray.

Leader Enfolded in the beauty of peace
let us pray to the Lord.
For those who are full of anger,
resentment and bitterness.

Silence

All Lord, fill them with your peace.

Leader For those who feel pressured,
over-worked and under-appreciated.

Silence

All Lord, fill them with your peace.

Leader For those who feel burdened with guilt
and who long for forgiveness.

Silence

All Lord, fill them with your peace.

Leader For those caught up in wars
and political unrest,
and live in constant fear.

Silence

All Lord, fill them with your peace.

Leader For the desperately lonely
who feel unwanted and unloved.

Silence

All Lord, fill them with your peace.

Leader God of Peace,

All Flow through us
and use us
as channels of your peace
for the peace of the world. Amen.

Sing *Make me a channel of your peace* **(35)**
Peace is flowing like a river **(46)**

Leader May the peace of God be with you.

All and may he also be with you.

Finish with a shared Peace.

7

God of Freedom

As you gather, sing *Bless the Lord, my soul* **(9)** until everyone is settled and joining in. Allow the singing to get quieter and quieter until God's silence can fill the gathering.

Leader 'If the Son sets you free,
then you will be really free.'

All If the Son sets us free,
then we shall be really free.

Silence Let your mind move over some of the many areas in our world where people are not really free. Think over some of the evils that trap, enslave and imprison them. Stand alongside them in their pain, in the presence of God.

Sing *Nada te turbe* **(39)**

Leader A reading from the Gospel of John.

Reading John 8.31-36

Leader This is the word of the Lord.
All Thanks be to God.
Leader Lord, we thirst for the freedom you offer;
All we thirst for your perfect freedom,
which shatters our prisons of self and sin,
and scatters the shadows
of failure and fear.
Lord, God of true freedom,
come; set us free.

Silence/Music
Music suggestion: Sibelius, *Symphony no. 6 (first movement)*. During this time, allow God to show you anything which is preventing you from living in his perfect freedom. Invite your Lord to break down all that still imprisons you and fetters your loving.

Sing *God forgave my sin* **(17)**

If we only seek peace **(20)**

8

Leader   Lord, when you set us free

All   you set us free to serve;

Leader   free to expend our lives

Women   in loving the hurt to wholeness,

Men   in supporting the weak,

Women   in striving for justice,

Men   in breaking down prejudice,

All   in washing one another's feet.

Leader   When you set us perfectly free

All   you set us free to serve.

Silence   Offer yourself for God to use as a means of bringing his freedom to others.

Leader   Wrapped, with all creation,
in the unlimited love of God,
let us share the aching hearts
of all who are denied basic human rights
and have no power and no voice.

　　　　Silence

All   Lord, set them free.

Leader   Let us share the pain of those who are
abused and tortured and imprisoned
for their conscience's sake.

　　　　Silence

All   Lord, set them free.

Leader   Let us share the grief
of those who must watch their children
die from starvation and disease.

　　　　Silence

All   Lord: set them free.

Leader   Let us share the joy of all who are freed
from pain, poverty and injustice;

All   and let us rejoice in all
whose generous lives
are poured out freely in love
for the good of the world. Amen.

Sing   *Make me a channel of your peace* **(35)**

Finish with a shared Peace.

9

God of Stillness

As you are gathering, sing *Be still, for the presence of the Lord* **(7)** until everyone is still and attentive to God.

Leader 'Be still and know that I am God.'

Silence Soak yourself in this silence. Don't spend it waiting for whatever comes next, but immerse yourself in the present moment. Absorb the stillness and silence until it is both around you and within you.

Leader In a world vibrating with action

All we have come here to be still.

Leader In a world of tight schedules
and deadlines

All we have come to absorb the present.

Leader In a world of limits and frustrations

All we have come to the brink of eternity.

Leader At the still point of our churning world

All we can meet the unchanging God
and know his peace.

Silence You may find it helpful to read over those words again, slowly and thoughtfully.

Sing   *Stay with me* **(49)**

Silence You are here in the heart of God's stillness. Don't force yourself to say anything or pray anything. Allow God to make his stillness deeply known in your body, your mind and your spirit.

Sing   *Let all that is within me* **(31)**

Leader Oh Lord, our God,

All you have created all things,
and you hold all things in existence.

Men Each moment is touched with your love,

Women each moment expresses your truth.

Leader Through time and eternity,

All YOU ARE. And we worship you.

Sing *In moments like these* **(21)**

Leader Listen, now, and hear the words of
Jesus, spoken to the Pharisees.

Reading John 8.56-58

Leader This is the word of the Lord.

All Thanks be to God.

Silence Recognise that all your past can be
brought into the everlasting presence of God;
offer him any memories which are painful,
so that he can heal them and transform them.

Sing *O Lord, your tenderness* **(44)**

Leader We pray now for all who need
God's stillness in their lives...
For those who are anxious about
many things; those for whom even little
worries loom very large.
Silence

All Lord, give them peace in your stillness.

Leader For those who have too much to do and
too little time to do it thoroughly.
Silence

All Lord, give them peace in your stillness.

Leader For those who are unnerved by solitude
and those who are desperately lonely.
Silence

All Lord, give them peace in your stillness;
give all of us your lasting peace. Amen.

Finish with a shared Peace.

—— God of Compassion ——

As people are gathering, sing *Bless the Lord, my soul* **(9)**. You are entering into ongoing worship, rather than hanging around waiting for a performance to start. As you arrive, settle into stillness and join in the singing when you are ready to.

Silence Think over the things in your life which you know need healing or changing. God has the power and the desire to rescue you.

Leader Lord, when we are still far off,

All you see us and run to welcome us.

Leader When we panic and start sinking,

All your arms are quick to hold us up.

Leader When we get lost and wander aimlessly,

All you never stop searching
until you have found us.

Leader And so we come to worship you,

All for you are our Good Shepherd,
and we are the sheep of your pasture.

Sing *Mon âme se repose* **(37)**

Leader Listen. Our God is among us
as he has promised. With love he reaches
out to us, person to person.

All Lord, we receive your love.

Silence Do not fill the silence with output to God. Be still in body and spirit and leave the output to God – allow your Lord to accept you and love you as his precious child.

Leader Listen now to these words from
Matthew's and Luke's Gospels.
Listen not only with your ears,
but with your heart as well.

1st Reading Matthew 9.35-36

Leader This is the word of the Lord.

All Thanks be to God.

2nd Reading Luke 5.12-13

Leader This is the word of the Lord.

All   Thanks be to God.

Silence/Music
Music suggestions: Lute, guitar or sitar pieces
which are thoughtful and unhurried in mood.
While you listen, remember times when you have
felt compassion for someone – a rush of love and a
longing to help them. Remember times when you
have been loved and rescued by someone.

Leader It is the very nature of our God to feel for
those in distress and long to help them.
So we bring to him now all those finding life
bewildering, chaotic and out of their control.

Silence

All   May they find shelter under your wings.

Leader We bring to him those who are disillusioned,
and have given up hope.

Silence

All   May they feel you reaching out to their need.

Leader We bring to you those who have been convinced
that they are not worth bothering with.

Silence

All   May they blossom, convinced that they are loved.

Leader We bring to you those who have been
taught by abuse never to trust.

Silence

All   May they be healed by your faithfulness.

Leader Lord, it is through our hands
That they will know your love;

All   God of compassion,forgive us for failing
to pass on the love you give us so freely.
Enable us and use us
to bring your love to the world. Amen.

Sing   *Spirit of the living God;* **(48)**
The King is among us; **(52)**

Leader As we have known the compassion of God,

All   we will strive to live with compassion
for all his sheep and lambs.

Finish with a shared Peace.

God of Wisdom

As you gather, sing *God be in my head* **(16)**.
This can be sung over several times, until everyone
is settled and attentive to God.

Silence   During this time acknowledge each thought
that floats up to the surface of your mind and 'hand
it over' to God. Allow his peace to fill your mind.

Leader   Lord, to whom else could we go?

All   You alone have the words of eternal life.

Leader   We ask you to open our minds
to greater possibilities;

All   to push back the margins
of our understanding.

Leader   To think your thoughts

All   and look with your eyes.

Leader   Oh Lord our God, to whom else could we go?

All   You alone have the words of eternal life.

Sing   *Misericordias Domini* **(36)**
Mon âme se repose **(37)**

Silence   Enjoy being in the companionship of the
God who knows you and loves you.

Leader   Listen and hear these words
from the book of Job.

Reading Job 28.12-28

Leader   This is the word of the Lord.

All   Thanks be to God.

Leader   There is so much in our world
to confuse and distress us;

All   so much that we do not understand.

Leader   You say that to be wise we need to have
reverence for the Lord of Wisdom.

All   To understand we need to turn from evil.

Leader We ask you, Lord, to help us see the evil
that is in our lives, and in our world.

All We ask you to give us courage to face it,
reject it and fight against it.

Silence Be relaxed yet alert, allowing your will to
be realigned to God's will, so that you are open to
receive any guidance, pricks of conscience or
reassurance from the God of Wisdom.

Leader Let us pray together now for a deeper
awareness of God's wisdom in our world...
For all whose lives
are confused and bewildering;
for those who can see no sense in life;

Silence

All Lord, may your wisdom
teach us understanding.

Leader For those who see God's wisdom
as foolishness; for those who entrust
their security to what is perishable;

Silence

All Lord, may your wisdom show us
where lasting treasure is found.

Leader For all in positions of authority
and responsibility, throughout the world.

Silence

All Lord, may your wisdom give
insight and integrity.

Leader For those who find it hard to make decisions;
for those paying dearly for past mistakes;

Silence

All Lord, may your wisdom work in us
for good, in every situation.

Leader Lord, God of Wisdom,

All Realign our minds and hearts and wills
to be at one with you,
in all we think, and feel and do. Amen.

Sing   *All heaven declares* **(3)**
Spirit of the living God **(48)**

Finish with a shared Peace.

God who Heals

As you gather, sing *Lay your hands gently upon us*
(30) , so that as people arrive they can join in.
Each time it is repeated, recognise, a little more
clearly, the wonder and healing power of God.

Silence Take time to be aware of how your body
is working automatically to keep you alive:
breathe naturally but notice the breathing; be
aware of your heartbeat, too.
Be thankful for being alive.

Leader Lord God, source of life,

All we rejoice that through the power
of your love we are alive;
breathing, thinking, feeling creatures,
made in your likeness
and for your glory.

Leader Lord God, source of life,

All recognising that our life exists
through your desire,
we thank you and praise you
and glorify you.

Sing *Laudate Dominum* **(29)**

Leader Listen now, both with ears and hearts,
to these words from Luke's Gospel.

Reading Luke 5.12-13

Leader This is the word of the Lord.

All Thanks be to God.

Silence Think over the reading. Imagine the
scene with the crowds, and all the colours, sights,
sounds and smells. Imagine how the leper was
feeling as he approached Jesus. Imagine how he
felt when he said to Jesus, 'If you want to you can
make me clean.' Think how encouraging and
loving Jesus is. Hear Jesus saying these words to
you: 'I do want to! Be clean.'

Leader Lord, it is always your will
to bring us to wholeness.

All We ask that your healing love
will enfold, soothe, support and comfort
all who are ill or in pain.

Leader Especially we pray for...

(Particular people can be named
before God. Time for prayer should be
given between each name –
they should not be read as a list.
Any of those present can feel free
to add other names.)

Sing *Oh Lord, hear my prayer* **(43)**

Silence During the next time of singing there can
be prayer ministry, anointing or laying on of
hands. Pray in this silence for those who will be
ministering God's love, and for those God is
longing to make whole and free.

Healing ministry, supported by prayer.

Suggested music:
Spirit of the living God **(48)**
Jesus, name above all names **(25)**
O let the Son of God enfold you **(42)**
Peace is flowing **(46)**
Do not be afraid **(12)**

As the healing ministry draws to a close:

Leader All praise and thanks be to our God
who loves us to wholeness!

All All praise and thanks be to our God,
to the Lord who saves us, Alleluia!

Finish with a shared Peace.

God who Listens

As you gather, sing *O Lord, hear my prayer* **(43)**
until everyone is drawn into the stillness in the
presence of God.

Silence Be aware of the stillness of your
surroundings – pillars; walls; windows – and yourself
as choosing to share stillness. Know that you and
your surroundings are held in being, in the present,
by the presence and will of God. Listen to the still
moment God has called you to share with him.

Leader In the confusion and noise of living

All you listen and hear our secret thoughts.

Leader Among the endless battering of words

All you listen and hear our unspoken longings.

Leader Through the barrage of anger
and misunderstanding

All you listen and hear the pain that we hide.

Women You hear the grieving of those
who are mourning;

Men you hear the joy of lovers and friends.

Women You hear the cheep of each sparrow
in danger;

Men you hear the bleat of each lamb who is lost.

Leader In our threats

All you hear our fear;

Leader in our jealousy

All you hear our cry to be valued;

Leader in our lack of forgiveness

All you hear our need to be forgiven.

Women And so we can come before you
in honesty and simplicity,

Men without pretence or exaggeration,

All for you have heard us already and know
our needs, our longings and our fears,
and we can trust you with what is most
precious to us – ourselves .

Silence Think over what you have been saying,
and trust God with your whole self. 'You are my
child, and I love you,' says the Lord.

Leader Some words to comfort us
          from Psalm 116, and Psalm 91.

Reading 1   Psalm 116.1-7
Reading 2   Psalm 91.14-16

Leader This is the word of the Lord.
All   Thanks be to God.

Silence/Music

Music suggestions: *Talk to me* from *His Light Shines*
(Kevin Mayhew). Listen to God welcoming you. In
the quietness, bring to him all that lies heavily on
your heart. Don't pretend, don't glamorise; unburden
everything in your own words, and just as it comes
to your mind.

Leader Let us pray together now
          for those who have no-one to talk to;
          no-one to turn to for sympathy or support.
          Silence

All   Lord, hear us, and supply our needs.
Leader We pray for all those who are misunderstood,
          and unfairly treated.
          Silence

All   Lord, hear us, and supply our needs.
Leader We pray for those who are deaf,
          and all who have difficulty speaking
          and making their needs understood.
          Silence

All   Lord, hear us, and supply our needs.
Leader We pray for those who feel powerless
          and ineffectual;
          those who are denounced for speaking out
          for what is right because it is unpopular.
          Silence

All   Lord, hear us, and supply our needs.
Leader We pray for all who are learning to speak,
          and all who are learning to pray.
          Silence

All   Thank you, Lord, for listening to us,
          both now and at all times.
          Help us to listen as you do:
          compassionately, open-mindedly, patiently,
          and with our whole attention. Amen.

Sing   *Make me a channel of your peace* **(35)**

Finish with a shared Peace.

God of Surrender

As you are gathering, sing *From heaven you came* **(14)**.

Silence Allow God to teach you about himself through the words, and music you have been singing and through the people around you whom he has chosen and called.

Leader Most holy God, the heavens and the earth
are full of your glory;
All all glory be to you, oh Lord most high!

Sing *All heaven declares* **(3)**; *Majesty* **(34)**

Silence Put aside all thoughts linked with yourself and your life, and focus your love and thankfulness on the God of glory. Worship him with your mind, your heart and your strength.

Leader All powerful Lord,
All we honour you;
Leader Lord of the universe and all creation,
All we offer you our praise.
Leader Lord of all time and distance,
All we worship and adore you.

Sing *Adoramus te, Domine* **(1)**

Silence It is not only those of you here now who are praising and adoring. You are part of a vast number, both on earth and in heaven, who are worshipping God because he is truly worthy of our worship.

Leader Listen now to a reading
from Paul's letter to the Philippians.

Reading Philippians 2.5-11

Leader This is the word of the Lord.
All Thanks be to God.
Leader Lord, we thank you
All that you were willing to surrender
everything, even your life, in order to
save us and set us free from sin.
Leader We thank you
All that you are Master, and yet you
come among us as one who serves.

20

Silence Think over all that the God of glory surrendered in order to become human and bring us abundant life. Think of the risks he took in doing so.

Sing *My song is love unknown* **(38)**

Leader Keeping in mind Christ's willingness
to surrender himself in complete obedience
to the way of Love, we pray...

All that we may be given courage
to relinquish our grip on what we possess,
so that we could gladly surrender
anything that might be required of us.
Silence

Leader We pray...

All that in our time, our talents and our
resources we may be more ready to give,
and more willing to share.
Silence

Leader We pray...

All that we may really place each day
at God's disposal, so that he can truly use
us in the way he needs to,
rather than in the way we choose.
Silence

Leader We pray...

All that whenever we are forced to surrender
our money, time or energy unexpectedly,
we may not grumble at the inconvenience,
but rejoice at the privilege.
Silence

Leader We pray...

All that you will enable us to give ourselves
completely away in order to enjoy
the richness of possessing Christ. Amen.

Silence Allow God to show you any parts of your life which have become too important to you; or any situations or people who need more of your time or resources than you are giving. Don't force this, making 'helpful' suggestions to God about it – you need only to be receptive to whatever he brings to mind.

Sing *If we only seek peace* **(20)**

Leader Let us go now
All in the power of the Lord; delighting in the
privilege of being no more than servants.

Finish with a shared Peace.

21

God of Reconciliation

As you gather, take a candle and light it, placing it round a globe or map of the world. While this is going on, everyone is singing *Jesus, remember me* **(24)**.

Silence During this quietness, think over these words, repeating them from time to time: 'Love your neighbour as yourself.'

Leader Man looks on the outward appearance

All but God looks on the heart.

Leader God knows us better
than we know ourselves;

All God understands us better
than we understand ourselves.

Women As a parent he watches us
take our first steps;

Men he is there, ready to pick us up
when we fall down.

Leader As our brother he has known
the cruellest temptation;

All as our Saviour he has power
to break our chains of sin.

Silence During the silence, call to mind one or two areas in your life where you have failed to keep the two great commandments – to love God, and to love your neighbour as yourself.

Leader Sin is a barrier which cuts us off from God.
Let us trust our Loving Father even with
the parts of us we are ashamed to admit.

All Loving Father, we are sorry
for all our barriers of sin
which block us off from you
and from each other.
We ask you to dissolve these barriers away,
and keep them down. Amen.

Sing   *Oh Lord, your tenderness* **(44)**
        Amazing grace **(4)**

Leader Listen to these words
from the first letter of John.

Reading 1 John 1.3-9

Leader This is the word of the Lord.

All Thanks be to God.

Silence/Music
Suggested music: Vivaldi, *The Four Seasons. (Spring,
no. 2, Largo).* During this time, reflect on the words
of the reading, accepting that God has completely
forgiven you – you are truly free, and are already
being healed of the damage sin has caused.

Leader Our world is greatly damaged by sin.
Let us pray together . . .
for those living together in strained
and difficult relationships;
for those brought up in an atmosphere
of mutual antagonism and distrust.
Silence

All Come among them, Lord, with your peace

Leader For long-standing family feuds
and unforgiven hurts;
for all who are rejected and insulted.
Silence

All Come among them, Lord, With your love

Leader For the gap of understanding between
those of different cultures, colours
and faiths; for our divided world.
Silence

All Come among us, Lord, with your openness

Leader Lord, we thank you

All that you have the power to reconcile
us to you and to each other.

Leader Lord, we ask you

All to keep us in this love,
ready to be servants
and peacemakers
whatever the personal cost. Amen.

Finish with a shared Peace.

God of Glory

As you gather, sing *Hosanna, hosanna* **(18)**;
Worthy, the Lord is worthy **(58)**. Pray the words as
you sing them, so that the singing is a true act of
praise and thanksgiving.

Leader   Glory to God!

All   Glory to God. Glory to God in the highest!

Sing   *Adoramus te, Domine* **(1)**

Silence   Delight in giving all honour and praise to
the only One in all time and space who deserves it.
You may find it helpful in starting you off to repeat
these words slowly and thoughtfully:

> Glory be to the Father
> and to the Son
> and to the Holy Spirit.
> As it was in the beginning,
> is now and shall be for ever. Amen.

Leader   Lord, how can we ever thank you enough
for all that you are
and all that you have done.

Women   We praise you for the wonder
of all that lives and grows;

Men   we praise you for pattern and order,
the complex and the simple.

All   The whole universe reflects your glory.

Women   From the wideness of space,

Men   to the detail of cells;

All   from the rainbow to the raindrop,
from the frog to the whale;
the whole universe reflects your glory,
and we worship you.

Silence/Music
Music suggestions: Vaughan Williams, *Orchestral
Fantasia 'Greensleeves theme'*; Dvorak, *Cello concerto
Op. 104 (second movement)*; Smetana, *Vltava from
Má Vlast*. Picture some of the landscapes of the world

you find especially beautiful or which have particularly special memories for you, and give God the praise and glory for them.

Leader A reading from Psalm 145.

Reading Psalm 145.1-13

Leader This is the word of the Lord.

All Thanks be to God.

Sing *This world you have made* **(54)**

Silence 'And we beheld his glory, the glory as of the only begotten Son of the Father, full of grace and truth.' Repeat these words from time to time as you think over the glory of God shown in the perfect loving, caring, healing life of Jesus.

Leader Let us pray together for the world
God loves so much.
For those who lavish affection on things
that can never fully satisfy;
Silence

All Lord, may your glory fill the earth.

Leader For those who have become
disillusioned with worldly values,
and have not yet discovered
where true value lies;
Silence

All Lord, may your glory fill the earth.

Leader For a misguided world which reckons
human worth in terms of
earning potential,
and parades greed as enterprise.
Silence

All Lord, may your glory fill the earth.

Leader Glorious in majesty, holy and almighty,

All we worship you, our Lord and God,
through time and through all eternity.
Amen.

Sing *I delight greatly in the Lord* **(19)**

Finish with a shared Peace.

God of Love

As everyone is gathering, sing *Ubi caritas* **(55)** until there is stillness, and attention is focused on the God of Love.

Silence As distractions drift up to the top of your mind, acknowledge them and put them to one side. As worries and anxious thoughts occur, hand them over to God. As feelings of guilt or regret emerge, tell God about it and let him know you are sorry. Allow him to forgive you.

Leader Wherever love is, there is God.

All What kind of love is God's love?

Women It is love that forgives

Men and then forgives

Women and forgives again.

Leader It is love that rolls up its sleeves

Women and gets involved with caring

Men and mending and building.

Leader It is love that is quite happy

Women to be considered a fool

Men to be considered weak.

All It is love that goes on giving but keeps no accounts; love that is non-selective and unconditional.

Leader This is the nature of God's love

All for this is the nature of our God.

Sing *Father, we adore you* **(13)**

Silence Thank God for the way he loves you unconditionally, even when he knows the worst as well as the best about you! Now bask in the warmth and affection of his love.

Leader Let us listen now to these words about the nature of love, from Paul's letter to the Christians in Corinth.

Reading 1 Corinthians 13.1-7

Leader This is the word of the Lord.

All Thanks be to God.

Sing   *A new commandment* **(6)**
       My song is love unknown **(38)**

Silence God is Love. Think over the reading about love, so as to understand more about the character of God.

Leader Lord, how amazing your love for us
           must be, since you were willing to
           become one with us
           and even to die for us.

All Lord, how amazing your love for us
      must be!

Sing   *Such love* **(50)**

Leader Knowing God's immense love for us all,
           let us bring to mind...
           All who are feeling unloved and unwanted.
           Silence

All Lord, let them know your love for them.

Leader All who are being taught to hate.
           Silence

All Lord, let them know
       your unconditional love.

Leader All who thirst for your faithful,
           accepting love, and do not realise
           it is freely available to them.
           Silence

All Lord, lead them to experience your love.

Leader All who, seeing only our poor example,
           reject the God we claim to serve.
           Silence

All Lord, may the light of our love so shine
      to others that they are drawn to know the
      joy of your love for themselves. Amen.

Sing   *Lord, the light of your love is shining* **(33)**

Finish with a shared Peace.

God of Joy

As you are gathering, sing *Jubilate Deo* **(27)**.
This can be sung as a round once enough people
have arrived.

Leader Thank you, Lord, our God,

All for the pleasure of your company;
for the companionship of your friends here;
for the happiness of singing
your praise together.

Leader Lord, we ask you

All to free us in our praise
so that we may enjoy to the full
receiving what you delight to give us,
and giving what you delight to receive.

Sing *I will enter his gates* **(23)**
Amen siakudumisa **(5)**
I delight greatly in the Lord **(19)**
Finish with *Can it be true* **(10)**

Silence Enjoy being in the company of your
Saviour, who is happy to share this time with you.
Talk with him if you wish, but you don't have to say
anything at all; it may help to think of yourself as a
young child just leaning against a loving parent.

Leader It was with joy that Mary sang;

All it was news of great joy
which the angels proclaimed.

Leader With joy the shepherd finds his lost sheep,

Women the woman her lost coin,

Men the ploughman his hidden treasure.

All The kingdom of God
is a kingdom of joy –
a deep delight which lasts for ever
and is for ever renewed;
a freshwater spring
that never runs dry.
Lord, give us this joy.

Silence The more we are turned in on ourselves, the less we will notice God's joy. Use this silence to turn deliberately away from self-centredness towards God-centredness. You will find any resentment, bitterness or annoyance beginning to lift; the space it leaves will be filled with God's joy.

Leader Lord, the joy that you provide

All is independent of mood, food or treats.

Women Your joy runs deeper than rapids;
it is beyond the range of all pain;

Leader your joy is promised
and brings great happiness;

All yet it is quite compatible with tears.

Leader Listen now to these words from Isaiah.

Reading Isaiah 35.1-10

Leader This is the word of the Lord.

All Thanks be to God.

Leader So let us pray together in the joy
and comfort of knowing God' s love
for us. . .
For all who weep and mourn at the moment.
Silence

All May their sorrow be turned into joy.

Leader For all who suffer from depression
and mental anguish.
Silence

All May their suffering be redeemed
and used for good.

Leader For those whose happiness
is dependent on status and money.
Silence

All May they know your lasting joy.

Leader For all who work to alleviate suffering.
Silence

All The fruit of the Spirit is love, joy,
and peace. May God, the source of hope,
fill us with all joy and peace. Amen.

Finish with a shared Peace.

——— God of Friendship ———

As you are gathering sing *Stay with me* **(49)**. As you arrive, join in with the ongoing worship when you are ready to.

Silence With thankfulness, think over some of your own friends and the qualities of their friendship which you really appreciate.

Leader Lord, we thank you

All for the companions you have given us
and the friendships we enjoy.

Women We thank you for those we can laugh
and cry with,

Men for those we relax with

All for those we are most comfortable with
because they accept us
and like us
as we are.

Leader Lord, we are sorry

All for the times we have let our friends down;
expected too much of them,
or too little.

Leader We are sorry

All that sometimes our selfishness
causes friction and sadness.

Leader Lord, we ask you

All to bless our friendships
and fill them
with your love.

Sing *Will you come and follow me* **(57)**

Silence Jesus calls us to be his friends – his companions. Are you willing to go with him? Allow God to remind you of some of the things which hold you back. Ask him to help you respond to his call.

Sing *I, the Lord of sea and sky* **(22)**

Leader   Listen. Hear these words of Jesus,
            from John's Gospel.
            Listen not only with your ears,
            but with your heart as well.

Reading John 15.10-17

Leader   This is the word of the Lord.

All   Thanks be to God.

Silence 'You are my friend if you do what I
command you . . . my command is that you love
one another.' Enjoy being in the company of
your Friend.

Leader   Jesus, our Saviour and our friend,
            we pray for all who are persecuted,
            sneered at, or ignored
            because they are your friends.
            Silence

All   Lord, may they know you are
            very close to them.

Leader   We pray for those
            who used to be your friends
            but who walk no longer
            in your company.
            Silence

All   Lord, may they be reminded of
            your love and faithfulness.

Leader   We pray for the children
            who are never introduced to you.
            Silence

All   Lord, may they be led to know you.

Leader   We pray for all who need befriending.
            Silence

All   Lord, make us instruments
            of your peace,
            so that many are drawn
            to know the joy of your friendship. Amen.

Finish with a shared Peace.

God of Journeys

As you gather, sing *O for a closer walk with God* **(40)**.
Join in with the singing as soon as you are ready,
and make sure the words go through your mind
before coming out of your mouth.

Silence Think over the promise Jesus has made
to you: 'Look, I am with you always; yes, to the
end of time.' It may help to repeat this over from
time to time as you let God show you how it affects
you and your life.

Leader We are a pilgrim people.

All A travelling people; followers of the Way.

Leader And 'I am the Way', says the Lord.

All Lord, not only do you lead the way;
you are the Way. Through you,
and in you, is the Way of love;
through you, and in you is the Way of life.

Sing *The Lord is my light* **(53)**

Silence Whatever the terrain of your life-journey,
you can walk it in the company of Jesus, so that
he becomes your route. Allow him to take over the
navigation from this moment. From now on, you
will be travelling on him, in him and with him.

Leader Lord, you have always led your people,
and travelled with them.

Women You called Abraham from the city to the desert;

Men Jacob discovered your closeness in his
loneliness as he fled from Esau;

All as Moses and the people of Israel
travelled in the wilderness,
you went before them always –

Women a pillar of cloud by day,

Men and by night a pillar of fire.

Leader No darkness is too dark for you;

All no depth or height is beyond your reach.

Leader You are there at our going out and our coming in

All from this time forward for evermore.

Sing   *Nada te turbe* **(39)**

Silence Think of the occasions and situations in
your life which you dread, and/or when you know
you are often tempted to behave unlovingly. Ask for
the Lord to protect and guide you through these
dangerous areas of your journey.

Leader We have God's promise
              that he will be with us always.
              Listen to these words of encouragement
              to us from the book of Isaiah.

Reading Isaiah 43. 1-7

Leader This is the word of the Lord.
All   Thanks be to God.

Silence Thank God for his promise, and know that
he will definitely keep it. Even through the valley
of the shadow of death you need not be afraid.
He will be with you, keeping you safe.

Leader Let us pray together now...
              For those who are coming near
              to the end of their earthly journey.
              Silence
All   Father, may they know the comfort
              of your presence.
Leader For those who have lost their way
              and can't get out of the mess
              they have got themselves into.
              Silence
All   Father, search for them, and carry them home.
Leader For those whose lives are at a crossroads,
              with important decisions
              to make about direction.
              Silence
All   Father, counsel them and show them the way.
Leader We thank you, Lord,
All   for your faithfulness and your constant love.
              As we journey, you are our strength
              and our song!

Sing   *O Jesus, I have promised* **(41)**

Finish with a shared Peace.

33

God of Hope

As you gather, sing *Jubilate Deo* **(27)** until everyone is settled and attentive to God. When everyone is there you can sing this chant in a round.

Silence Think over some of the things about our world which make you feel sad, or which disturb you. Think of areas where you feel powerless to change things for the better.

Leader Lord, in our weakness,

All we come to you for strength.

Leader In our blindness,

All we come to you for sight.

Leader In our desire for good to be accomplished,

All we come to you,
the source of all goodness.

Leader In our longing for the coming
of the Kingdom,

All we approach you, the King of kings.

Leader Lord, our God,

Women your light dispels all darkness,

All your springs make deserts blossom;

Leader the warmth of your love

Women melts what is frozen,

Men restores what was lost

All refreshes what was weary.

Leader In you, Lord God, there is always hope,

All because you have overcome sin and death,
and opened to us the gates of heaven.

Sing *Such love* **(50)**; *Just as I am* **(28)**

Silence In the peace of this stillness, still your body and mind. Allow God to fill you with his peace; peace of mind and peace of spirit. Things may seem hopeless to us, but 'with God all things are possible'.

Leader Listen now to these words
from Paul's letter to the Ephesians.

Reading Ephesians 1.11-20

Leader This is the word of the Lord.

All   Thanks be to God.

Silence Hope is not a doubtful wish; it is a joyful
certainty about the future. Ask that God will
increasingly open your mind to see this hope
which he has called you to.

Sing   *Open our eyes, Lord* **(45)**; *Do not be afraid* **(12)**

Leader Heavenly Father, knowing that you love us,
we come to you with
our needs and concerns.
We bring to your love
our desire for deeper faith,
and a clearer understanding
of your will for us.
Silence

All   Lord, you are our hope and our strength.

Leader We bring to your love our reluctance to
trust you and our longing to trust you more.
Silence

All   Lord, you are our hope and our strength.

Leader We bring to your love all who rely
and depend on us,
and our concern not to let them down.
Silence

All   Lord, you are our hope and our strength.

Leader We bring to your love the areas of our life
which have become too precious to us,
and our desire to serve you alone.
Silence

All   Lord, you are our hope and our strength,
and we put our trust in you.

Sing   *Nada te turbe* **(39)**

Finish with a shared Peace.

God of Sorrow

As you gather, sing *Jesus, remember me* **(24)** until everyone is attentive to God, in stillness.

Silence We are bound to have brought here with us some of the pressure and busy-ness of life. Allow God to quieten not just your body, but your mind and spirit as well. Breathe IN his peace; breathe OUT all hurry and tension.

Leader Lord, we lay at your feet

All all that we are,
all that we have been,
and all that we could become.

Leader Because we can come to you honestly,

All and because we can trust you
not to reject us,
we have come to confide in you
our secret pains and sorrows,
our nagging doubts, and regrets,
and our deepest fears.

Silence/Music
Suggestion for music:
Mozart, *Clarinet Concerto (slow movement).*
Confide in the God who made you, understands you and loves you. Tell him about those things which weigh heavily on your heart.

Leader Listen now to these words
from the book of Isaiah.

Reading Isaiah 53.1-6

Leader This is the word of the Lord.

All Thanks be to God.

Leader The God we worship
is also the man of sorrows,
and acquainted with grief.

All He shares in the depth
of each personal sorrow;

Men	he shares in the deepest darkness of pain;
Women	he shares in the anguished face of the tortured,
All	the starving, the rejected, the oppressed.
Leader	So, Lord, in our sorrow
All	we cry to you for help;
Women	for the exhausted and the lonely,
Men	for the crippled and the weak;
Women	for the frightened and the slandered,
Men	for the desperate and the poor.
All	Lord, in mercy, come to our aid.

Sing   *O Lord, hear my prayer* **(43)**

Leader   Hear, now, these words of comfort
from Paul's letter to the Romans.

Reading Romans 8. 35-39

Leader   This is the word of the Lord.

All   Thanks be to God.

Silence   Think over the amazing power and capacity
of God's love for you. It is large enough to take the
suffering of every person in every generation. Lean
on that love, and allow it to sustain and refresh you.

Sing   *Adoramus te, Domine* **(1)**

Leader   Immeasurably power must your love be,
O Lord;

All   willingly taking our suffering upon you;
dying that we may be brought to new life.
Lord, may we thank you and praise you
for ever, both in our words,
and the way that we live.

Leader   Lord, anoint us to love with your loving,
sharing one another's burdens
and bearing the light of your hope
to the world. Amen.

Sing   *You shall go out with joy* **(60)**

Finish with a shared Peace.

God of Unity

While you are gathering, sing *Jesu tawa pano* **(26)** until everyone is settled and attentive to the Lord God, in whose honour you have come.

Silence It takes time to become 'collected', even within ourselves. By focusing your attention on these words: 'Jesus, we are here for you', allow your body, your mind and your spirit to be united in worshipping God.

Leader Jesus, you have drawn us here,

All from different places
and from different backgrounds,
to unite us in your love.

Leader Lord, we acknowledge

All that in many ways our lives lack unity.

Men Between the ideals and the pressures

All there is compromise;

Women between the dreams and the realities

All there are frustrations;

Leader between the belief and the expression

All there is misunderstanding and conflict.

Leader So, Lord, we turn to you to unite us;

All to whom else could we go?
You alone have the words of eternal life!
As we centre our lives on you,
melt our divisions and make us one.

Sing *Agios O Theos* **(2)**; *O Lord, your tenderness* **(44)**

Silence Don't try to fill this space with thoughts, however holy. Hold yourself still, relaxed but attentive, so that God can fill you and work his healing in you.

Leader Let us listen now to part of Jesus' prayer
for the apostles, just before he was crucified.

Reading John 17. 11b-23

Leader This is the word of the Lord.

All Thanks be to God.

Sing *Bind us together, Lord* **(8)**

Leader Brothers and sisters in Christ,
let us pray together...
For the millions, all over the world,
who have come to know Jesus as Lord.
Silence

All May we all be one,
as you and the Father are one.

Leader For the leaders and pastors
of the different churches.
Silence

All May we all be one, as you
and the Father are one.

Leader We thank you for the joy of worshipping
together, and the privilege of serving
the same Master.
Silence

All May we all be one, as you
and the Father are one.

Leader We offer you every opportunity
for praying and working together,
so that you can use us to your glory.
Silence

All May we all be one, as you
and the Father are one.

Leader By your arms outstretched in love
for us on the cross,

All draw us to love and forgive one another;
draw us to be less thrown
by our difference, and more encouraged
by what we hold in common.

Leader Breathe through us, Holy Spirit,

All renew us and revive us,
until all people come to worship you. Amen.

Sing *Laudate Dominum* **(29)**

Finish with a shared Peace.

—— God who is Persecuted ——

As you are gathering, sing *Stay with me* **(49)**.When you arrive, join in with the ongoing worship as soon as you are ready.

Silence You may think you are here just because you decided to come. But you are also here because God chose you to be. Be still and attentive to him now.

Leader	We have come to spend time watching and praying with Christ.
All	Lord, in the garden of Gethsemane you asked your friends to watch with you and pray.
Leader	In agony of spirit you prayed,
Men	knowing the terrible ordeal that was before you;
Women	knowing the hate in the eyes of those who wanted you dead;
All	knowing the vulnerability of love.
Leader	'Greater love has no man than this,
All	that he will lay down his life for his friends.'

Silence Imagine that agony of Gethsemane. Be relaxed in your body and alert in your spirit, so that you can watch and pray with the persecuted Christ.

Sing   *My song is love unknown* **(38)**

Leader Listen to this great teaching of Jesus about persecution and suffering.

Reading Matthew 5.3-12

Leader This is the word of the Lord.
All   Thanks be to God.

Silence Do you rejoice when you are ridiculed or insulted on account of following Jesus? Let the full impact of this teaching take root in you, until you can consider any such antagonism, however small, a great privilege.

Leader Loving is always expensive.
All   When we love, we put ourselves at risk;
            we are no longer insulated
            against pain and rejection.
            Loving is an expensive way to live.

40

Leader Loving is also rewarding.

All No other way fulfils us;
no other way gives us peace and joy.
Only love can set our lives free.

Sing *Do not be afraid* **(12)**; *Give thanks* **(15)**

Silence You will be given all the strength and resources you need for doing God's will. Allow him to equip you now for whatever he has in mind for you to do and be.

Leader Let us pray together now...
For all children who are badly treated,
neglected or abused.
Silence

All Lord, as their suffering wounds you,
may it also wound us to work
for their protection and comfort.

Leader For the mentally retarded,
and the simple minded, who are vulnerable,
and easy prey to the unscrupulous.
Silence

All Lord, as you understand their needs,
and care for them, may we, too,
understand their needs and care for them.

Leader For all whom society prefers to ignore.
Silence

All Lord, as you consider each one precious,
may we, too, consider each person precious.

Leader For the cruel and hard-hearted;
for all who abuse, destroy and undermine.
Silence

All Lord, as you forgave those
who persecuted you, may we, too,
forgive our enemies, and pray for them.

Leader For all who are the victims of war,
terrorism, and political injustice.
Silence

All Lord, may we recognise your face in the face
of everyone who is persecuted;
help us to realise that when we respond
with love to the least of these,
we shall be responding to you. Amen

Sing *Take my hands* **(51)**

Finish with a shared Peace.

God of Refreshment

As you are gathering, sing *Come, Holy Ghost* **(11)**; *Just as I am* **(28)**. Join in with the singing as soon as you are settled in stillness.

Silence Recognise in this quietness, in God's attentive presence, the things you lack and need in your spiritual life. You can be quite honest with God about these – nothing is beyond his compassion or his forgiveness.

Leader Lord, you alone can
supply our deepest needs;
All you alone can satisfy and fulfil.
Leader Come, Holy Spirit of God,
All come and fill us to overflowing.

Sing *Veni, Sancte Spiritus* **(56)**

Silence Remind yourself that to God you are very precious; well-known and well-loved. He knows your needs – even those which you may not be aware of. Imagine yourself as a pilgrim, footsore and weary. Jesus is looking after you with care and refreshment.

Leader Listen now to the words of Psalm 23,
which speak to us of the courteous
and sensitive way that God refreshes us
and caters for our needs.

Reading Psalm 23

Leader This is the word of the Lord.
All Thanks be to God.

Sing *O let the Son of God enfold you* **(42)**

Silence Let the love of God enfold you. For this moment, nothing else is so important. If thoughts filter up to distract you, just acknowledge them and put them to one side. For the moment they don't have priority. Let God's enfolding love envelop your body, your mind and your spirit.

Leader Anyone who trusts in the Lord

All is like a tree planted by the waterside;

Leader it thrusts out its roots into the stream

All and is untroubled by heat or drought.

Leader So the Lord says,
'Come to me, all you who are thirsty;
come to me and I will refresh you'.

Leader Lord, we pray . . .
For all in need of refreshment in their faith;
for those whose prayer life
is dry and parched.

Silence

All Lord, may they drink
from your living water.

Leader For those who are overwhelmed
with doubts and misgivings about the
faith in which they have been brought up.

Silence

All Lord, as they drink from your living water
may they find the reality of your presence
for themselves.

Leader For those actively involved in ministry;
that they may be given space and time
to receive your necessary refreshment.

Silence

All Lord, refresh them for their ministry
and for their own spiritual growth.

Leader For all of us here today,
and for those we spend time with
each day.

Silence

All Lord, you open your arms to welcome us,
and refresh us with many good things;
supplied with your gifts,
and empowered by your love,
may our lives tell others
the Good News that can give life;
life in abundance! Amen.

Sing *Amen siakudumisa* **(5)**

Finish with a shared Peace.

43

—— God of Encouragement ——

While you are gathering, sing *Yesuve saranam* **(59)**
with a cantor, and everyone else repeating each
phrase. As you sing this Indian song, feel solidarity
with Christians in other continents.

Silence Make yourself aware of the different parts of
your body, and relax them, one by one. Concentrate
on the present moment; remember that it is held in
being by God, and surrender to him your whole self.

Leader 'Fear not, little flock,
it is the Father's good pleasure
to give you the Kingdom.'

All Lord, we thank you that time and again
you encourage us on our journey.

Leader Whenever weakness overtakes us,

Men whenever your will seems blocked,

Women whenever the next step looks treacherous,

All whenever we reach the limits
of our resources;

Leader then you encourage and strengthen
our resolve,

Men you show us that with you
all things are possible,

Women you support us during the difficult moves,

All and provide for our every need.

Leader Oh Lord, our God,

All without your encouragement
we would so often give up;
we thank you for empowering us
to work for the coming of your Kingdom.

Sing *Lord of my life* **(32)**

Silence Think over the times God has given you
encouragement at low points of your life – through
a friendship, or words spoken, or a particular event,
or an experience of his presence in prayer.
Thank God for such personal loving care.

Leader Listen now to these words
of encouragement from Luke's Gospel.

Reading Luke 12. 22-32

Leader This is the word of the Lord.
All Thanks be to God.

Sing *Nada te turbe* **(39)**

Leader Knowing that our heavenly Father
loves and cares for all he has created,
let us pray to him now...
For those who are feeling discouraged,
and those who are experiencing failure.
Silence

All Lord, give them your encouragement.
Leader For those who are wary
of stepping out in faith.
Silence

All Lord, give them your encouragement.
Leader For those whose self-esteem is low,
and those who are despised.
Silence

All Lord, give them your encouragement.
Leader For those weakened
by lives which are burdened
with crisis after crisis.
Silence

All Lord, give them your encouragement.
Leader Lord, you have promised us
All that you will be with us always,
to the end of the world.
With that promise to encourage us
in every situation,
may we walk your way with joy,
and infect the world with hope. Amen.

Sing *You shall go out with joy* **(60)**

Finish with a shared Peace.

God of Humility

When you arrive, settle yourself in God's presence,
and join in the singing which is already going on –
Be still, for the presence of the Lord **(7)**.

Silence Take time to tame your active mind to
stillness. Keeping a relaxed but expectant stillness
in your body is of value here; breathe naturally
and regularly, and think of yourself breathing IN
God's peace with every breath.

Leader Lord, we live in the middle
of your remarkable creation;

All all around us there is evidence
of your power, your glory
your wisdom and your love.

Leader And yet you came among us
as one who serves;

All instead of lording it over us,
you stand patiently at our door and knock.

Leader Instead of imposing your presence on us,

All you wait to be invited.

Leader So now we invite you, Lord;

All come to us; abide with us for ever.

Silence In the opportunity of this unhurried
quietness, invite God to live in you and through
you, both now and for the future. Use your own,
natural words, and remember that although
God is unnervingly powerful, he is also full of love
and gentleness.

Sing *In moments like these* **(21)**

Leader We do love you, Lord,

All knowing that you first loved us

Leader In your humility you show us

All the love that puts others before ourselves;
the love that has given self completely away;
the love that holds each one precious,
and treats each one with respect.

Leader   Listen now to these words
from Mark's Gospel.

Reading Mark 10.35-45

Silence   Think over any areas where you may need
to change your attitudes, in the light of this
teaching. Ask the Lord to show you what these
areas are, and empower you to realign your values
where necessary.

Leader   Let us pray together now...
For all who are in positions of authority.
Silence

All   Lord, make us content to do only
your will.

Leader   For those who have others
dependent on them.
Silence

All   Lord, make us content
to do only your will.

Leader   For those who live in terror
because of political or
personal victimisation.
Silence

All   Lord, in our weakness,
give us your strength.

Leader   For those whose countries
are held in poverty
through others' self-indulgence.
Silence

All   Lord, knowing our reliance
on you for everything,
and following your example
of loving service, may we receive
your strength and will to practise the
simplicity of humility,
in everything we do and say,
everywhere we go. Amen.

Sing   *Amazing grace* **(4)**

Finish with a shared Peace.

God of Power

As you are gathering, sing *Agios o Theos* **(2)**; *Be still, for the presence of the Lord* **(7)**, until everyone is attentive to the God of power and holiness. When you arrive, add your voice to the praise.

Silence   Recognise that you are in the presence of the One who created the entire universe; the One who sees and understands all things.

Sing   *Adoramus te, Domine* **(1)**

Silence   In this time of silent adoration, worship the Lord your God with all your mind and with all your heart and with all your strength. Don't allow anything to distract you from this essential duty and joy.

Leader   Maker of all;
All   sustainer of all;
Men   we worship you,
Women   we adore you,
All   for you are our God.
Leader   When I look at the sky,
which you have made,
at the moon and the stars,
which you set in their places –
All   what is man, that you think of him;
mere man, that you care for him?

Silence   Think over the different aspects of our universe which remind you of God's power – perhaps as a waterfall; a thunderstorm; a volcano; the beginning of a new star. Think, too, of the power over sin and disease that Jesus showed.

Leader   O Lord, our Lord,
All   your greatness is seen in all the world!

Sing   *This world you have made* **(54)**

Leader   Listen now to these readings,
which tell of people's reaction
to being shown God in the power of his glory.

Reading 1   Ezekiel 3. 22-24 (Ezekiel, the prophet)
Reading 2   Luke 2. 8-10 (The shepherds)
Reading 3   Matthew 17.1-7 (Peter, James and
                 John at the transfiguration)
Reading 4   Acts 2. 6-11 (Paul at his conversion)

Leader This is the word of the Lord.

All Thanks be to God.

Silence God still acts with great power in people's lives. Some find the thought of this terrifying. Do you hold back from him through fear? Remember that the God of power is also the God of love. 'Do not be afraid'.

Sing   *Do not be afraid* **(12)**

Leader Let us pray together now in the presence
          of the almighty God who loves us...
          For a deeper understanding
          of the Lord of time and space.
          Silence

All Lord, have mercy on us.

Leader For light to see more clearly
          our need of God.
          Silence

All Lord, have mercy on us.

Leader For the courage to allow God
          access to every corner of our lives.
          Silence

All Lord, have mercy on us.

Leader For the humility to give God the glory
          for all that he does through us.
          Silence

All Lord, have mercy on us.

Leader Lord, we thank you

All for the privilege of spending
          this time in your presence.

Leader We offer you now

All the strength, the time and the resources
          that you have given us. Take us, Lord,
          and use us for your glory. Amen.

Sing   *Take my hands* **(51)**

Finish with a shared Peace.

God of Acceptance

While you are gathering, sing *Yesuve saranam* **(59)** until everyone is settled in the presence of God. As you arrive, join in with the singing as soon as you are ready to.

Silence Think of the different roles you play in your life – you may be a child to one person, a parent to another, and employer to one, a friend to another. Accept all these aspects of yourself, and come before God, who sees all, hiding nothing and inventing nothing about yourself.

Leader Lord we praise you

All that in order to save us
you accepted the limitations of humanity;
in order to set us free
you accepted death by crucifixion;
in order to redeem us
you accepted the need
to pay the price for sin
in full,
and without condition.

Leader Oh Lord, our God,

All we thank you, and adore you.

Sing *Can it be true* **(10)**

Silence In thankfulness, think over the accepting love shown in Jesus, which carried on forgiving right through torture and execution; and continues forgiving us now, right through the times we reject his commands, ignore his will, or forget to honour him.

Leader Lord, not only did you accept death
in obedience to the Way of love;

All but you also accept us,
just as we are,
and in full knowledge
of what we could be.

Leader   Listen now to these words of God,
spoken both
to the chosen people of Israel
and also to us, the new Israel.

Reading Isaiah 43.1-7

Leader   This is the word of the Lord.
All   Thanks be to God.

Sing   *If we only seek peace* **(20)**

Silence   In stillness, allow God to nourish you,
so that in accepting him as Lord of your life,
you can love as he loves.

Leader   Lord, let your will be done in us
and in your world.
Show us where we have not yet
fully accepted your ways.
Silence
All   Lord, let your will be done in us.
Leader   Bless the work of all peacemakers,
and all involved in practical loving care.
Silence
All   Lord, let your will be done in us.
Leader   Encourage us when we discover
that acceptance of your Way
leads us to the cross.
Silence
All   Lord, let your will be done in us.
Leader   Lord, when we fail you,
do not give up on us;
when we turn away,
turn us back to you.
Silence
All   Lord, let your will be done in us.

Sing   *I delight greatly in the Lord* **(19)**
or
A new commandment **(6)**

Finish with a shared Peace.

51

——— God of Creation ———

As you are gathering, sing *Jubilate Deo* **(27)**. When enough people are present, you can sing as a round if you like.

Leader Lord of creation,
All   we rejoice in all that you have made;
         heaven and earth are full of your glory!

Silence Run your mind over some of the most beautiful places you have visited, or seen in pictures or on film. Think of them as the works of an artist, and let your pleasure in God's world lead you on to worship the artist himself.

Sing   *This world you have made* **(54)**

Leader Out of the darkness and void,
All   God is creating.
Leader Out of chaos,
All   God is bringing order.
Leader Out of the fragments we offer,
All   God is creating wholeness.
Leader Into despair,
All   God breathes hope:
Leader into anxiety,
All   God breathes peace:
Leader into deadness,
All   God breathes life.

Silence With your body still and relaxed, but attentive, notice the stillness of things around you and feel part of the present moment, which is held in place by God's love.

Sing   *Let all that is within me* **(31)**

Leader Listen now to these words
         from John's Gospel.

Reading John 1.1-14

Leader This is the word of the Lord.

All Thanks be to God.

Silence Think over the words you have been
listening to: 'In the beginning was the Word: the
Word was with God and the Word was God'. Jesus,
then, is the Word of God; the Expression of God.

Leader Heavenly Father, in Jesus we have seen
your glory with a human face.
Through Jesus we pray...
For the world you have created
in all its beauty and variety.
Silence

All Lord, make us good stewards
of all your gifts.

Leader For the regions of rich growth
and for the parched deserts,
with all the life they need to support.
Silence

All Lord, make us good stewards
of all your gifts.

Leader For the life you have given us,
with our particular responsibilities
and opportunities.
Silence

All Lord, make us good stewards
of all your gifts.

Leader For our families, friends and neighbours,
and all who provide for our needs.
Silence

All Lord, make us good stewards
of all your gifts.

Leader Lord of creation,

All we offer you our lives;
we ask that we may be
instruments of praise,
in the words we speak,
in the things we do,
in the way that we live. Amen.

Sing *Amen siakudumisa* **(5)**

Finish with a shared Peace.

———— God of Eternity ————

While you are gathering, sing *Misericordias Domini* **(36)**
until everyone is settled and joining in the praise of
God's everlasting loving kindness.

Silence Try to put aside all thoughts of the past
and the future. Be attentive to the present moment,
where you are in stillness, in the company of your
Lord and Saviour.

Leader Before and after time,

All   there is God.

Leader Where past and future are gathered,

All   there is God.

Leader Beyond the death of the body,

All   there is God.

Leader For you, O Lord, are everlasting,

All   faithful for ever and eternally present;
           You are the great 'I AM' and we worship you.

Sing   *Jesus, name above all names* **(25)**
          Majesty **(34)**
          Jesu tawa pano **(26)**

Silence When we worship God we are living not
only in time but in eternity as well. In this time of
quietness, recognise this amazing truth, and know
yourself to be in both dimensions, entirely through
the grace and love of the everlasting God.

Leader Along with all who worship God,
           both in this world and in heaven,

All   we give you the glory and praise
           which you alone deserve.

Leader Though we are all of us separate
           in this moment of time,

All   in colour, in shape, and in place;

Leader Yet, through the power of the God we worship,

All   we are united in one body, and one spirit,
           bound together in time and eternity.

Silence Take time to feel solidarity with other Christians in different countries and in different cultures, all over the world. They are all your brothers and sisters. You are their brother or sister. Remember this as you pray in the silence: 'OUR Father in heaven, may your name be hallowed.'

Leader Listen now to John's gospel.

Reading John 8. 54-58

Leader This is the word of God.

All Thanks be to God.

Leader My brothers and sisters in Christ,
let us pray now to the God
who lives for ever...
We remember with gratitude
those we have loved and who have now
passed through death into eternity.
Silence

All You are the resurrection, and you are life.

Leader We remember those
who are approaching death,
and commit them
to your everlasting love and mercy.
Silence

All you are the resurrection, and you are life.

Leader We remember those who
are fearful of dying,
and those who are fearful of staying alive.
Silence

All you are the resurrection, and you are life.

Leader We remember the whole company
of believers who have ever,
and will ever live;

All with them we praise and glorify the Lord
who is alive,
and reigns for ever as our eternal King.
Blessed be God for ever!

Sing *Ubi caritas* **(55)**

Finish with a shared Peace.

God of Growth

As you are gathering, sing *Open our eyes, Lord* **(45)** followed by *Lord of my life* **(32)**. When you arrive, settle yourself to stillness and join in with the ongoing worship.

Silence Think of yourself strongly rooted, like a tree, with your roots sunk into the deep spring of God, which will never run dry. Draw inner life and peace from that spring now.

Leader 'Blessed is anyone who trusts in the Lord;
All such a person is like a tree by the waterside, that thrusts its roots to the stream:
Leader when the heat comes it has nothing to fear, its foliage stays green;
All untroubled in a year of drought, it never stops bearing fruit.
Leader Lord, deepen our trust,
All that in you we may grow strong and bear much fruit.'

Sing *If we only seek peace* **(20)**

Silence Think over your own life in the light of what you have been singing. Ask God to show you any branches of behaviour that need pruning; and any roots that you rely on, which lead only to puddles that will run dry. Allow God to nurture strong growth in you.

Leader Listen now to these words of Jesus.

Reading John 15.1-8

Leader This is the word of the Lord.
All Thanks be to God.
Leader Lord, in all your creation
Women we see the profusion of growth;
Men the variety of fruits:
All the cycle of regeneration.

56

Leader In every acorn

All there is the potential for a forest;

Leader in every apple pip

All there is the potential for an orchard;

Leader in every soul

All there is the potential for your kingdom,
to be established,
full of peace, and joy, and love.
O Lord, may your kingdom come,
in us and in all creation.

Silence In the attentive stillness, long for the
Kingdom of God to come in you and in the
whole world.

Leader Let us pray together
for the growth of the kingdom . . .
For many hearts to be alerted
to their need of God, and fullness of life
that he alone can give.
Silence

All Lord, may your kingdom come.

Leader For all who have put their trust
in money, possessions and success,
and feel the nudge of disillusion.
Silence

All Lord, may you kingdom come.

Leader For those in whom spiritual growth
is fragile and vulnerable.
Silence

All Lord, may your kingdom come.

Leader The growing may be painful;

All root-growth may be unseen;

Leader we may sometimes prefer the seed we are

All to the tree we might become.

Leader Lord, give us courage for the growing,

All that we may grow tall in your love
and bear fruit in abundance for your glory,
and for the good of your world. Amen.

Sing *Will you come and follow me* **(57)**

Finish with a shared Peace.

57

God of Order

As everyone is gathering, sing *Majesty* **(34)**; *God be in my head* **(16).** When you arrive, settle to stillness in the presence of God, and join in the ongoing worship.

Silence As you breath IN, think of yourself drawing in God's gift of life; as your breath OUT, think of yourself exhaling all concern with Self. Breathe naturally and regularly.

Leader Lord, we owe our entire existence
to your constant love for us.

All In you alone we live and move
and have our being.

Women Our genetic inheritance,

Men our genetic functioning;

All all is designed and sustained
by the mastery of your hands
and the power of your love.

Leader Not only in our own bodies,
but throughout the whole of creation,

All there is order and pattern,
structure and design,
balance and beauty.

Leader O Lord, our God,
how excellent are your ways:

All let everything that has breath
praise the Lord!

Sing *Worthy, the Lord is worthy* **(58)**

Silence Let your whole being – body, mind and spirit – give thanks and praise to the God who designed you, made you and sustains your life, along with all living creatures throughout the world.

Leader Listen now to these words from Psalm 104,
rejoicing in the mastery
and caring nature of God.

Reading Psalm 104.24-33

Leader This is the word of the Lord.

All Thanks be to God.

Leader Let us praise together
the God who brings order out of chaos.
We praise him for all the times
that good has emerged
from evil in our lives,
and difficulties have been overcome.

Silence

All Lord, we thank you, and praise you.

Leader We praise him for every argument
that has been resolved;
and every relationship
which has been healed.

Silence

All Lord, we thank you and we praise you.

Leader We praise him for each time
that confusion
has given way to understanding;
and fear to reassurance.

Silence

All Lord, we thank you and we praise you.

Leader We praise you, Lord,

All for every time
the weak are treated with gentleness,
the lonely with affection,
the distressed with sympathy,
and the downtrodden with respect.

Leader Your ways, Lord, are perfect;

All may our lives,
ordered according to your will,
proclaim the beauty of your peace. Amen.

Sing   *Take my hands* **(51)**

Finish with a shared Peace.

—— God who Protects ——

While everyone is gathering, have *The Lord is my light* **(53)** already being sung, so that as you arrive, you settle yourself into stillness in the presence of God, and join in the ongoing worship.

Silence Here in the company of your Lord, you can let all your tension go, because you are completely safe. Slowly and deliberately, let yourself relax in the everlasting arms of the One who loves you, now and for ever.

Leader   In many ways the psalmists express
         their wonder at God's protection:
All   Lord, open our hearts to understand
         the wonder of your love for us.
Leader   The Lord covers us with his feathers;
All   we find shelter under his wings.
Leader   The Lord is a strong rock;
All   he provides firm footing
         so that our feet do not slip.
Leader   The Lord pulls us out of deep water;
All   in the mire of our distress he rescues us.
Leader   We need only to say, 'I am slipping',
All   and the Lord is there to hold us up.
Leader   Lord, however can we thank you
All   for your constant loving-kindness
         and faithful care of us.

Sing   *The King is among us* **(52)**

Silence Know that in your heavenly Father's eyes, you are his special child – accepted and loved. No matter how old you are, or how often you have failed or been rejected by others, your heavenly Father knows you personally by name, and he loves you.

Leader   Listen now to these words from
         Matthew's Gospel, where, through Jesus,
         we are shown God's loving protection.

Reading Matthew 14. 22-33

Leader This is the word of the Lord.

All Thanks be to God.

Silence/Music
Music suggestion: Greig, *Peer Gynt suite: ('Morning').*
Imagine yourself during the violent storm, in that
boat with the disciples. Imagine yourself walking
over the pounding waves to Jesus. What goes
through your mind as you feel yourself sinking?
How do you feel as Jesus catches hold of you and
brings you to safety? Notice how calm the sea has
become. How do you feel about Jesus now?

Leader Knowing that our heavenly Father
holds each person in his love,
let us pray...
For those in various parts of the world
who are in danger at the moment
from war and terrorism.

Silence

All Lord, protect them;
keep them eternally safe.

Leader For the young and vulnerable
who are sleeping rough
in cities throughout the world.

Silence

All Lord, protect them;
keep them eternally safe.

Leader For all children whose mental,
physical or emotional health
is endangered by abuse or neglect.

Silence

All Lord, protect them;
keep them eternally safe.

Leader O Lord our God, we rejoice
that whatever happens to us,

All nothing at all can ever separate us
from the love of God
which is in Christ Jesus our Lord.
Alleluia!

Sing *Jesus, name above all names* **(25)**

Finish with a shared Peace.

God of Faithfulness

While everyone is gathering, sing *I will enter his gates* **(23)** and *Lord of my life* **(32)**. As you arrive, settle your mind and body, and join in with the worship when you are ready.

Leader God has promised us
that where two of three are gathered together
in his name, he will be there amongst them.

All Holy God, help me draw near to worship you
with all my heart,
and with all my mind,
and with all my strength.

Silence Offer the Lord your full attentiveness. Let your body be relaxed, and breathe naturally and regularly. Every thought that filters up can be turned into worship by offering it to God. Let the Lord himself teach you and empower you to worship in the best way.

Sing   *Give thanks* **(15)**

Leader Lord, we give you thanks
and we praise you,

All for in spite of our weakness
and in spite of our poverty,
you are always faithful in your love for us.

Leader Though we let you down,
and turn away from your presence,

All yet you never ever forget us,
never give up on us, never stop loving us.

Silence Hear in your mind this great promise that the Lord makes to you: 'Look, I am with you always'. Let the words take root in you, not just for now, but for the situations and relationships in your life where Jesus' presence would make all the difference.

Leader Listen now to these words of the psalmist,
praising God for his faithfulness
and abiding love.

Reading Psalm 103

Leader   This is the word of the Lord.

All   Thanks be to God.

Leader   As children of our loving heavenly Father,
let us pray together...
For those who feel let down or slighted
by someone they love;
for all whose faithfulness
is being severely tested.

    Silence

All   Lord, increase our faith,
and keep us faithful.

Leader   For those who find it hard to believe
in a completely faithful God;
all who are afraid to trust
in case they are let down.

    Silence

All   Lord, increase our faith,
and keep us faithful.

Leader   For those who have wandered
so far from your way,
that they feel themselves
beyond your forgiveness and love.

    Silence

All   Lord, increase our faith,
and keep us faithful.

Leader   In stillness, let us dedicate ourselves again
to following the Lord faithfully
each day of our lives.

Silence You may find it helpful to use these words of St. Patrick:

> *Lord, may I know you more clearly*
> *love you more dearly*
> *and follow you more nearly*
> *day by day.*

Or use your own words. It is not the words, but the longing and the love which are important.

Sing   *Bind us together, Lord* **(8)**

Finish with a shared Peace.

————— God of Patience —————

As you are gathering, sing *Agios o Theos* **(2)**. When you arrive, settle yourself to stillness and join in the worship.

Silence Think over with sadness the many ways you are unworthy of the patient love of God. Lay these times before him and ask his forgiveness.

Sing   *O Lord, your tenderness* **(44)**

Silence Take time to accept the Lord's forgiveness and be assured of his continuing love for you. Allow God to make you into the kind of person he hopes you will become.

Leader Lord, you are so patient with us;
Women so often we lag behind your will,
            or race ahead with our own plans;
Men   so often we do the right things
            for the wrong reasons,
            and fail to obey your will.
All   Yet time and again you search us out
            and find us, time and again you forgive us
            and bring us safely home.
Leader Most patient Saviour,
All   we love you and adore you.

Sing   *In moments like these* **(21)**

Leader Listen now to these words of Peter in
            his second letter, and James in his letter.

Reading 1   2 Peter 3. 8-9
Reading 2   James 5. 7-11

Leader This is the word of the Lord.
All   Thanks be to God.

Silence We tend not to think too much about the time when Jesus will come again in glory. Spend time now to reflecting on the knowledge that it will certainly happen, and all we know about the date is that we will not be expecting it. How ready are you for this? Are you prepared for it every day?

Leader Let us pray together
for the coming of the Kingdom...
That we may live each day
as if it were our last.

Silence

All Lord, be patient with us
and teach us your ways.

Leader We pray for a more accepting love,
so that we may be more patient
with those who annoy and irritate us.

Silence

All Lord, be patient with us
and teach us your ways.

Leader We pray for those whom we irritate
and annoy, and ask for sensitivity in
recognising our own faults
and weaknesses.

Silence

All Lord, be patient with us
and teach us your ways.

Leader We pray for your blessing and anointing
on all who need patience in their work.

Silence

All Lord, be patient with us
and teach us your ways.

Leader Lord, through our sufferings

All teach us to persevere
and put our trust in you;

Leader through any unjust criticisms
for doing your will,

All teach us patient and joyful acceptance.

Leader As we run the race that is set before us,

All Let us run with patience,
delighting only in doing your will.

Sing   *Do not be afraid* **(12)**

Finish with a shared Peace.

Hymns

1

Adoramus te, Domine.

We adore you, O Lord.
(Taizé)

2

Agios o Theos,
agios ischiros,
agios athanatos,
eleison imas.

Holy God,
holy and mighty,
holy and immortal,
have mercy on us.
(Traditional)

3

1. All heaven declares
the glory of the risen Lord.
Who can compare
with the beauty of the Lord?
For ever he will be
the Lamb upon the throne.
I gladly bow the knee
and worship him alone.

2. I will proclaim
the glory of the risen Lord,
who once was slain
to reconcile man to God.
For ever you will be
the Lamb upon the throne.
I gladly bow the knee
and worship you alone.
(Noel and Tricia Richards)

4

1. Amazing grace! How sweet
the sound
that saved a wretch like me.
I once was lost, but now
I'm found:
was blind, but now I see.

2. 'Twas grace that taught
my heart to fear,
and grace my fears relieved.
How precious did that
grace appear
the hour I first believed.

3. Through many dangers,
toils and snares

I have already come.
'Tis grace hath brought me safe
thus far,
and grace will lead me home.

4. The Lord has promised
good to me
his word my hope secures.
He will my shield and portion be
as long as life endures.
(John Newton, 1725-1807)

5

Amen siakudumisa!
Amen siakudumisa !
Amen bawo.
Amen bawo.
Amen siakudumisa !

Amen. Praise the name
of the Lord!
(Traditional)

6

A new commandment I
give unto you:
that you love one another
as I have loved you,
that you love one another
as I have loved you.

By this shall all men know
that you are my disciples —
if you have love one for another
(Repeat)
(Author unknown,
based on John 13. 34-35)

7

1. Be still, for the presence of the
Lord, the Holy One is here
Come, bow before him now,
with reverence and fear.
In him no sin is found, we stand
on holy ground.
Be still, for the presence of the
Lord, the Holy One is here

2. Be still, for the glory of the Lord
is shining all around;
he burns with holy fire,
with splendour
he is crowned.
How awesome is the sight,
our radiant King of light!

Be still, for the glory of the Lord
    is shining all around.

3. Be still, for the power of the Lord
    is moving in this place,
he comes to cleanse and heal,
    to minister his grace.
No work too hard for him, in faith
    receive from him;
be still, for the power of the Lord
    is moving in this place.
(Dave Evans)
© 1986 Thankyou Music

8

Bind us together, Lord,
bind us together
with cords that cannot be broken.
Bind us together, Lord,
bind us together,
bind us together with love.

1. There is only one God,
there is only one King.
There is only one Body,
that is why we sing:

2. Made for the glory of God,
purchased by his precious Son,
born with the right to be clean,
for Jesus the victory has won.

3. You are the family of God,
you are his promise divine,
you are God's chosen desire,
you are the glorious new wine.
(Bob Gillman)
© 1977 Thankyou Music

9

Bless the Lord, my soul,
and bless his holy name.
Bless the Lord, my soul;
he rescues me from death.
(Taizé)
© 1984 Ateliers et Presses de Taizé

10

1. Can it be true, the things
    they say of you?
You walked this earth
    sharing with friends
you knew all that they had,
    the work, the joy, the pain,
that we might find the way
    to heav'n again.

2. And day by day you still
    return this way;
but we recall there was a debt
    to pay:

out of your love for your own
    world above
you left that holy thing,
your endless love to prove.

3. Can it be true, the things
    they did to you—
the death, the shame,
and were your friends so few?
Yet you returned again
    alive and free—
can it be true, my Lord?
    It had to be!
(Brother William)
© Allans Publishing (Australia) Pty. Ltd.

11

1. Come, Holy Ghost,
    our souls inspire,
and lighten with celestial fire;
thou the anointing Spirit art,
who dost thy sevenfold
    gifts impart.

2. Thy blessed unction from above
is comfort, life, and fire of love;
enable with perpetual light
the dullness of our blinded sight.

3. Anoint and cheer our soilèd face
with the abundance of thy grace:
keep far our foes,
    give peace at home;
where thou art guide
    no ill can come.

4. Teach us to know the
    Father, Son,
and thee, of both, to be but one;
that through the ages all along
this may be our endless song:

5. 'Praise to thy eternal merit
Father, Son and Holy Spirit.'
    Amen.
(John Cosin, 1594-1672 , after an
anonymous 9th Cent. Latin hymn)

12

Do not be afraid,
for I have redeemed you.
I have called you by your name;
you are mine.

1. When you walk
    through the waters,
    I'll be with you.
You will never sink
    beneath the waves.

2. When the fire is burning
    all around you,
    you will never be consumed
    by the flames.

3. When the fear of loneliness
    is looming,
    then remember I am at your side.

4. When you dwell in the exile
    of the stranger,
    remember you are precious
    in my eyes.

5. You are mine, O my child;
    I am your Father,
    and I love you with a perfect love.
    (Gerard Markland,
    based on Isaiah 43. 1–4)
    © 1978 Kevin Mayhew Ltd

13

1. Father, we adore you,
    lay our lives before you.
    How we love you!

2. Jesus, we adore you . . .

3. Spirit, we adore you . . .
    (Terry Coelho)
    © 1972 Maranatha! Music USA

14

1. From heaven you came,
    helpless babe,
    entered our world,
    your glory veiled;
    not to be served
    but to serve,
    and give your life
    that we might live.

    This is our God,
    the Servant King;
    he calls us now
    to follow him,
    to bring our lives
    as a daily offering
    of worship to
    the Servant King.

2. There in the garden
    of tears,
    my heavy load
    he chose to bear;
    his heart with sorrow
    was torn,
    'Yet not my will
    but yours,' he said.

3. Come see his hands
    and his feet,
    the scars that speak

of sacrifice,
hands that flung stars
into space
to cruel nails
surrendered.

4. So let us learn
    how to serve,
    and in our lives
    enthrone him;
    each other's needs
    to prefer,
    for it is Christ
    we're serving.
    (Graham Kendrick)
    © 1983 Thankyou Music

15

Give thanks with a grateful heart.
Give thanks to the Holy One.
Give thanks because he's given
Jesus Christ, his Son.

And now let the weak say,
'I am strong',
let the poor say,
'I am rich',
because of what the Lord
has done for us. *(Repeat)*

Give thanks.
(Henry Smith)
© 1978 Integrity's Hosanna! Music

16

God be in my head, and in
    my understanding;
God be in mine eyes,
    and in my looking;
God be in my mouth,
    and in my speaking;
God be in my heart,
    and in my thinking;
God be at mine end,
    and at my departing.
(Book of Hours, 1514)

17

1. God forgave my sin
    in Jesus' name.
I've been born again
    in Jesus' name.
And in Jesus' name I come to you
to share his love as he told me to.

    He said: 'freely, freely
    you have received,
    freely, freely give.
    Go in my name,
    and because you believe,
    others will know that I live.'

2. All pow'r is giv'n in Jesus' name,
   in earth and heav'n
         in Jesus' name.
   And in Jesus' name I come to you
   to share his pow'r
         as he told me to.

3. God gives us life in Jesus' name,
   he lives in us in Jesus' name.
   And in Jesus' name I come to you
   to share his peace
         as he told me to.
   (Jimmy and Carol Owens)

18

1. Hosanna, hosanna,
   hosanna in the highest.
   (Repeat)
   Lord, we lift up your name.
   with hearts full of praise;
   be exalted, O Lord my God!
   Hosanna in the highest!

2. Glory, glory,
   glory to the King of kings!
   (Repeat)
   Lord, we lift up your name
   with hearts full of praise;
   be exalted, O Lord my God!
   Glory to the King of kings!
   (Carl Tuttle,
   based on Matthew 21.9)

19

I delight greatly in the Lord,
My soul rejoices in my God.
(Repeat)
For he has clothed me
with garments of salvation
and arrayed me
in a robe of righteousness.
(Repeat)
(Chris Bowater,
based on Isaiah 61.10)

20

1. If we only seek peace
   when it's to our advantage,
   if we fail to release
   the down-trodden and poor,
   then let the gen'rous caring,
   boundless sharing of the God
   who walked this earth
   nourish our roots until we fruit
   in the joy of the Lord.

The story of love he came to tell us,
bound in the making of the world.
We are the pages still unwritten:
let the story be told.

2. If we try to avoid
   inconvenient giving,
   or if love is destroyed
   by our failure to serve
   then let the wide, unflinching,
         selfless giving
   of the God who walked this earth
   nourish our roots until we fruit
   in the joy of the Lord.

3. If we start to object
   to the path we are given
   and decide to select
   other ways of our own,
   then let the full acceptance,
         firm obedience
   of the God who walked this earth
   nourish our roots until we fruit
   in the joy of the Lord.
   (Susan Sayers)

21

In moments like these
      I sing out a song,
I sing out a love song to Jesus.
In moments like these
      I lift up my hand,
I lift up my hands to the Lord:
singing 'I love you, Lord',
singing 'I love you, Lord',
singing 'I love you, Lord,
I love you'.
(David Graham)

22

1. I, the Lord of sea and sky,
   I have heard my people cry.
   All who dwell in dark and sin
   my hand will save.
   I who made the stars of night,
   I will make their darkness bright.
   Who will bear my light to them?
   Whom shall I send?

   Here I am, Lord. Is it I, Lord?
   I have heard you calling
         in the night.
   I will go Lord, if you lead me.
   I will hold your people in my heart.

2. I, the Lord of snow and rain,
   I have borne my people's pain.
   I have wept for love of them.
   They turn away.
   I will break their hearts of stone,
   give them hearts for love alone.
   I will speak my word to them.
   Whom shall I send?

3. I, the Lord of wind and flame,
   I will tend the poor and lame.
   I will set a feast for them.
   My hand will save.
   Finest bread I will provide
   till their hearts be satisfied.
   I will give my life to them.
   Whom shall I send?
   (Dan Schutte S.J. from Isaiah 6)
   © 1981 Daniel L. Schutte and New Dawn Music

23

I will enter his gates with
    thanksgiving in my heart,
I will enter his courts with praise.
I will say, 'This is the day that the
    Lord has made.'
I will rejoice for he has
    made me glad.
He has made me glad, he has
    made me glad,
I will rejoice for he has
    made me glad.
He has made me glad, he has
    made me glad,
I will rejoice for he has
    made me glad.
(Leona von Brethorst)
© 1976 Maranatha! Music USA

24

Jesus, remember me
when you come
into your Kingdom.
(Taizé)
© 1981 Ateliers et Presses de Taizé

25

Jesus, name above all names.
Beautiful Saviour, glorious Lord;
Emmanuel, God is with us,
blessed Redeemer, living Word.
(N. Hearn)
© 1974, 1979 Scripture in Song/Thankyou Music

26

Jesu tawa pano;
Jesu tawa pano;

Jesu tawa pano;
tawa pano mu zita renyu.

> *Jesus, we are here;*
> *Jesus, we are here;*
> *Jesus, we are here;*
> *we are here for you.*
(Patrick Matsikenyiri)
© Patrick Matsikenyiri

27

Jubilate Deo, omnis terra.
Servite Domino in laetitia.
Alleluia, alleluia in laetitia.
Alleluia, alleluia in laetitia.

> *Rejoice in God, all the earth.*
> *Serve the Lord with gladness.*
(Taizé)
© 1981 Ateliers et Presses de Taizé

28

1. Just as I am, without one plea
   but that thy blood
       was shed for me,
   and that thou bidst me
       come to thee,
   O Lamb of God, I come.

2. Just as I am, though tossed about
   with many a conflict,
       many a doubt,
   fightings and fears within,
       without,
   O Lamb of God, I come.

3. Just as I am, poor,
       wretched, blind;
   sight, riches, healing of the mind,
   yea, all I need, in thee to find,
   O Lamb of God, I come.

4. Just as I am, thou wilt receive
   wilt welcome, pardon,
       cleanse, relieve:
   because thy promise I believe,
   O Lamb of God, I come.

5. Just as I am (thy love unknown
   has broken every barrier down),
   now to be thine, yea, thine alone,
   O Lamb of God, I come.

6. Just as I am, of that free love
   the breadth, length, depth,
       and height to prove,
   here for a season, then above,
   O Lamb of God, I come.
   (Charlotte Elliott, 1789-1871)

29

Laudate Dominum,
laudate Dominum omnes gentes,
alleluia!

Praise the Lord, all
peoples, alleluia!
(Taizé)
© 1981 Ateliers et Presses de Taizé

30

Lay your hands gently upon us,
let their touch render your peace,
let them bring your forgiveness
and healing,
lay your hands, gently lay
your hands.

1. You were sent to free
       the broken-hearted.
   You were sent to give
       sight to the blind.
   You desire to heal all our illness.
   Lay your hands, gently lay
       your hands.

2. Lord, we come to you through
       one another,
   Lord, we come to you
       in all our need.
   Lord, we come to you
       seeking wholeness.
   Lay your hands gently,
       lay your hands.
   (Carey Landry)
   © 1977 North American Liturgy Resources

31

1. Let all that is within me cry: Holy.
   Let all that is within me cry: Holy.
   Holy, holy, holy, is the Lamb
       that was slain.

2. Let all that is within me cry:
       Mighty . . .

3. Let all that is within me cry:
       Worthy . . .

4. Let all that is within me cry:
       Blessed . . .

5. Let all that is within me cry:
       Jesus . . .
   (Traditional)

32

1. Lord of my life,
       the ground of my being
   great energy charged

with the stillness of peace.
Lost in the wonder
of all you encompass
the rest of my life
I lay at your feet.

2. Lord of my joy,
   clear stream of refreshment,
   profusion of love
   like blossom in spring.
   Lost in the wonder
   of all you encompass
   my fears and my cares
   to your goodness I bring.

3. Lord of my strength,
   the source of all healing,
   your purity deep
   as the green ocean's floor.
   Lost in the wonder
   of all you encompass
   I ask only this —
   to be yours evermore.
   (Susan Sayers)
   © 1984 Kevin Mayhew Ltd

33

1. Lord, the light of your love
       is shining,
   in the midst of the darkness,
       shining,
   Jesus, Light of the world,
       shine upon us,
   set us free by the truth
       you now bring us,
   shine on me, shine on me.

   Shine, Jesus, shine,
   fill this land with the
       Father's glory;
   blaze, Spirit, blaze,
   set our hearts on fire.
   Flow, river, flow,
   flood the nations with
       grace and mercy;
   send forth your Word, Lord,
   and let there be light.

2. Lord, I come to your awesome
       presence,
   from the shadows into
       your radiance;
   by the blood I may enter
       your brightness,
   search me, try me, consume all
       my darkness.
   Shine on me, shine on me.

71

3. As we gaze on your
      kingly brightness
so our faces display
      your likeness,
ever changing from glory to glory,
mirrored here may our lives
      tell your story.
Shine on me, shine on me.

(Sing refrain twice to end)
(Graham Kendrick)
© 1987 Make Way Music

34

Majesty, worship his majesty;
unto Jesus be glory,
honour and praise.
Majesty, kingdom, authority
flow from his throne
      unto his own:
his anthem raise.
So exalt, lift upon high
the name of Jesus;
magnify, come glorify
Christ Jesus the King.
Majesty, worship his majesty,
Jesus who died, now glorified
King of all kings.
(Jack Hayford)
© Rocksmith Music

35

1. Make me a channel of your peace.
Where there is hatred,
      let me bring your love.
Where there is injury,
      your pardon, Lord.
And where there's doubt,
      true faith in you.

2. Make me a channel of your peace.
Where there's despair in life,
      let me bring hope.
Where there is darkness
      only light,
and where there's sadness
      ever joy.

3. O, Master, grant that I may
      never seek
so much to be consoled
      as to console,
to be understood
      as to understand,
to be loved, as to love,
      with all my soul.

4. Make me a channel of your peace.
It is in pardoning
      that we are pardoned,
in giving to all men
      that we receive,
and in dying that we're born
      to eternal life.
(Sebastian Temple, based on the
Prayer of St. Francis of Assisi)
© 1966 Franciscan Communications

36

Misericordias Domini
in aeternum cantabo.

> *I will sing for ever of the*
>   *mercy of the Lord*
(Taizé)
© 1981 Ateliers et Presses de Taizé

37

Mon âme se repose
en paix sur Dieu seul:
de lui vient mon salut.
Oui, sur Dieu seul
mon âme se repose,
se repose en paix.

> *On God alone my soul rests*
> *in peace; from him comes*
>   *my salvation.*
(Taizé)
© Ateliers et Presses de Taizé

38

1. My song is love unknown,
my Saviour's love to me,
love to the loveless shown,
that they might lovely be.
O who am I, that for my sake,
my Lord should take
      frail flesh and die?

2. He came from his blest throne,
salvation to bestow;
but men made strange, and none
the longed-for Christ would know,
but O, my friend,
      my friend indeed,
who at my need his life did spend!

3. Sometimes they strew his way,
and his sweet praises sing;
resounding all the day
hosannas to their King;
then 'Crucify!' is all their breath,
and for his death they thirst
      and cry.

4. Why, what hath my Lord done?
   What makes this rage and spite?
   He made the lame to run,
   he gave the blind their sight.
   Sweet injuries! Yet they at these
   themselves displease,
       and 'gainst him rise.

5. They rise, and needs will have
   my dear Lord made away;
   a murderer they save,
   the Prince of Life they slay.
   Yet cheerful he to suffering goes,
   that he his foes from thence
       might free.

6. Here might I stay and sing,
   no story so divine;
   never was love, dear King,
   never was grief like thine.
   This is my friend in whose
       sweet praise
   I all my days could gladly spend.
   (Samuel Crossman, c. 1624-84)

39

Nada te turbe,
nada te espante:
quien a Dios tiene
nada le falta.
Nada te turbe,
    nada te espante:
solo Dios basta.

> *Let nothing trouble you,*
> *let nothing frighten you:*
> *whoever has God lacks*
>   *nothing.*
> *God alone is enough.*

(Taizé)
© Ateliers et Presses de Taizé

40

1. O for a closer walk with God,
   a calm and heavenly frame;
   a light to shine upon the road
   that leads me to the Lamb.

2. Return, O holy Dove, return,
   sweet messenger of rest:
   I hate the sins that made
       thee mourn,
   and drove thee from my breast.

3. The dearest idol I have known,
   whate'er that idol be,

help me to tear it from thy throne,
and worship only thee.

4. So shall my walk be close
       with God,
   calm and serene my frame;
   so purer light shall mark the road
   that leads me to the Lamb.
   (William Cowper, 1731-1800)

41

1. O Jesus, I have promised
   to serve thee to the end;
   be thou for ever near me,
   my Master and my Friend:
   I shall not fear the battle
   if thou art by my side,
   nor wander from the pathway
   if thou wilt be my guide.

2. O let me feel thee near me:
   the world is ever near;
   I see the sights that dazzle,
   the tempting sounds I hear;
   my foes are ever near me,
   around me and within;
   but, Jesus, draw thou nearer,
   and shield my soul from sin.

3. O let me hear thee speaking
   in accents clear and still,
   above the storms of passion,
   the murmurs of self-will;
   O speak to reassure me,
   to hasten or control;
   O speak, and make me listen,
   thou guardian of my soul.

4. O Jesus, thou hast promised
   to all who follow thee,
   that where thou art in glory
   there shall thy servant be;
   and, Jesus, I have promised
   to serve thee to the end:
   O give me grace to follow,
   my Master and my Friend;

5. O let me see thy foot-marks,
   and in them plant mine own;
   my hope to follow duly
   is in thy strength alone:
   O guide me, call me, draw me,
   uphold me to the end;
   and then in heaven receive me,
   my Saviour and my Friend.
   (John E. Bode, 1816-74)

42

1. O let the Son of God enfold you
   with his spirit and his love,
   let him fill your heart and satisfy
       your soul.
   O let him have the things that
       hold you,
   and his Spirit, like a dove,
   will descend upon your life
       and make you whole.
   Jesus, O Jesus, come
       and fill your lambs. (twice)

2. O come and sing this song
       with gladness
   as your hearts are filled with joy;
   lift your hands in sweet
       surrender to his name.
   O give him all your tears
       and sadness,
   give him all your years of pain,
   and you'll enter into life in
       Jesus' name.
   (John Wimber)
   © 1979 Mercy Publishing/Thankyou Music

43

O Lord, hear my prayer,
O Lord, hear my prayer:
when I call answer me.
O Lord hear my prayer,
O Lord, hear my prayer:
come and listen to me.
(Taizé)
© Ateliers et Presses de Taizé

44

O Lord, your tenderness,
melting all my bitterness,
O Lord, I receive your love.
O Lord, your loveliness,
changing all my ugliness,
O Lord, I receive your love.
O Lord, I receive your love,
O Lord, I receive your love.
(Graham Kendrick)
© 1986 Thankyou Music

45

Open our eyes, Lord,
we want to see Jesus,
to reach out and touch him
and say that we love him;
open our ears Lord,
and help us to listen.
O open our eyes, Lord,
we want to see Jesus!
(Robert Cull)
© 1976 Maranatha! Music USA

46

1. Peace is flowing like a river,
   flowing out through you and me,
   spreading out into the desert,
   setting all the captives free.

2. Love is flowing like a river . . .

3. Joy is flowing like a river . . .

4. Hope is flowing like a river . . .
   (Author unknown)

47

1. Peace, perfect peace, is the gift of
       Christ our Lord. *(2)*
   Thus, says the Lord, will the
       world know my friends.
   Peace, perfect peace, is the gift of
       Christ our Lord.

2. Love, perfect love . . .

3. Faith, perfect faith . . .

4. Hope, perfect hope . . .

5. Joy, perfect joy . . .
   (Kevin Mayhew)
   © 1976 Kevin Mayhew Ltd

48

1. Spirit of the living God,
       fall afresh on me.
   Spirit of the living God,
       fall afresh on me.
   Melt me, mould me,
       fill me, use me.
   Spirit of the living God,
       fall afresh on me.

2. *Repeat verse 1 singing 'us'*
       instead of 'me'.
   (Michael Iverson)

49

Stay with me,
remain here with me,
watch and pray,
watch and pray.
(Taizé)
© 1984 Ateliers et Presses de Taizé

50

Such love! Such grace!
makes the pieces
come falling into place,
breaks through the darkness,
turns on the light,
making blindness
give way to sight.
Your love has conquered,
has set us free

to become all
you've called us to be,
healing the wounded,
making us stand,
bringing peace and a sword
in our hand.
And no power in the universe
can separate us
from the love of God.
We're yours forever
with nothing to fear,
willing slaves to the love
that brought us here.
*(Dave Bryant,based on
Romans 8. 39)*

51

1. Take my hands
   and make them as your own,
   and use them for your Kingdom
       here on earth.
   Consecrate them to your care,
   anoint them for your
       service where
   you may need your gospel
       to be sown.

2. Take my hands.
   They speak now for my heart,
   and by their actions they will
       show their love.
   Guard them on their daily course,
   be their strength and guiding
       force
   to ever serve the Trinity above.

3. Take my hands.
   I give them to you, Lord.
   Prepare them for the service
       of your name.
   Open them to human need
   and by their love they'll
       sow your seed
   so all may know the love
       and hope you give.
   (Sebastian Temple)

52

1. The King is among us,
   his Spirit is here,
   let's draw near and worship,
   let songs fill the air.

2. He looks down upon us,
   delight in his face,
   enjoying his children's love,
   enthralled by our praise.

3. For each child is special,
   accepted and loved,
   a love gift from Jesus
   to his Father above.

4. And now he is giving
   his gifts to us all,
   for no one is worthless
   and each one is called.

5. The Spirit's anointing
   on all flesh comes down,
   and we shall be channels
   for works like his own.

6. We come now believing
   your promise of power,
   for we are your people
   and this is your hour.

7. The King is among us,
   his Spirit is here,
   let's draw near and worship,
   let songs fill the air.
   (Graham Kendrick)

53

The Lord is my light,
My light and salvation;
in him I trust,
in him I trust.
(Taizé)

54

*This world you have made
    is a beautiful place:
it tells the pow'r of your love.
We rejoice in the beauty
    of your world,
from the seas to the
    heavens above.*

1. The morning whispers of purity;
   the evening of your peace;
   the thunder booms your
       exuberance
   in the awesome pow'r you release.

2. The tenderness of a
       new-born child;
   the gentleness of the rain;
   simplicity in a single cell;
   and complexity in a brain.

3. Your stillness rests
       in a silent pool;
   infinity drifts in space;
   your grandeur straddles
       the mountain tops;

and we see your face
in each face.
(Susan Sayers)

55

Ubi caritas et amor,
Ubi caritas Deus ibi est.

> *Where there is charity*
> *and love,*
> *there is God.*

(Taizé)

56

Veni, Sancte Spiritus.

> *Come, Holy Spirit.*

(Taizé)

57

1. Will you come and follow me
   if I but call your name?
   Will you go where you don't know
   and never be the same?
   Will you let my love be shown,
   will you let my name be known,
   will you let my life be grown,
   in you and you in me?

2. Will you leave yourself behind
   if I but call your name?
   Will you care for cruel and kind
   and never be the same?
   Will you risk the hostile stare
   should your life attract or scare?
   Will you let me answer prayer
   in you and you in me?

3. Will you let the blinded see
   if I but call your name?
   Will you set the prisoners free
   and never be the same?
   Will you kiss the leper clean
   and do such as this unseen,
   And admit to what I mean
   in you and you in me?

4. Will you love the 'you' you hide
   if I but call your name?
   Will you quell the fear inside
   and never be the same?
   Will you use the faith
   you've found
   to reshape the world around,
   through my sight and
   touch and sound
   in you and you in me?

5. Lord, your summons echoes true
   when you but call my name.
   Let me turn and follow you
   and never be the same.
   In your company I'll go
   where your love and
   footsteps show.
   Thus I'll move and live and grow
   in you and you in me.
   (Scottish Traditional))

58

1. Worthy, the Lord is worthy,
   and no one understands
   the greatness of his name.
   Gracious, so kind and gracious,
   and slow to anger and rich,
   so rich in love.

   > *My mouth will speak in praise*
   > *of my Lord,*
   > *let every creature praise*
   > *his holy name.*
   > *For ever and ever more.*
   > *(4 times)*

2. Faithful, the Lord is faithful
   to all his promises, and loves
   all he has made.
   Righteous, in all ways righteous,
   and he is near to all who call
   on him in truth.
   (Ian White, based on Psalm 122)

59

Yesuve saranam,
saranam Yesuve.

> *Jesus, I surrender.*

(Traditional)

60

You shall go out with joy
and be led forth with peace,
and the mountains and the hills
shall break forth before you.
There'll be shouts of joy
and the trees of the field
shall clap, shall clap, their hands,
and the trees of the field
shall clap their hands,
and the trees of the field
shall clap their hands,
and the trees of the field
shall clap their hands,
and you'll go out with joy.
(S. Dauermann)

Acknowledgements

The publishers wish to express their gratitude to the following for permission to use copyright material in this book:

Ateliers et Presses de Taizé, F-71250 Taizé-Communauté, France for: *Mon âme se repose; Nada te turbe; O Lord hear my prayer.*

Boosey & Hawkes, 295 Regent Street, London W1R 8JH for *Freely, freely* © Copyright 1972 Lexicon Music Inc. All rights for the UK & Eire administered by United Nations Music Publishing Ltd.

Franciscan Communications, 1229 South Santee Street, Los Angeles, California 90115, USA for *Make me a channel of your peace* © Copyright 1966 and *Take my hands* © Copyright 1966.

Harper Collins, 77-85 Fulham Palace Road, London W6 8JB for *Jesus remember me; Misericordias Domini; Laudate Dominum; Adoramus te, Domine; Jubilate Deo omnes terra; Ubi caritas* and *Veni Sancte Spiritus* from *Music from Taizé Volume I*, and *Stay with me; Bless the Lord, my soul; The Lord is my light* from *Music from Taizé Volume II.*

The International Bible Society, 1820 Jetstream Drive, Colorado Springs, C080921, USA for *Worthy, the Lord is worthy* from the Holy Bible, New International Version © Copyright 1973, 1978, 1984.

Integrity's Hosanna! Music, PO Box 16801, Mobile, AL36616, USA for *Give thanks* © Copyright 1978.

Iona Community, Pearce Institute, 840 Govan Road, Glasgow G51 3UT for *Will you come and follow me* © 1987 Wild Goose Publications.

Leosong Copyright Management Ltd, 7-8 Greenland Place, London NW1 OAP on behalf of Rocksmith Music for *Majesty* © Copyright 1976.

Patrick Matsikenyiri, Zimbabwe for *Jesu tawa pano.*

North American Liturgy Resources, 10802 North Twenty-Third Avenue, Phoenix, Arizona 85029, USA for *Lay your hands* © Copyright 1977. All rights reserved.

New Dawn Music Inc., 5536 N.E. Hassalo, Portland, Oregon 97213, USA for *I the Lord of sea and sky.* © 1981 Daniel L. Schutte and New Dawn Music.

Stainer & Bell Ltd, PO Box 110, 82 High Road, East Finchley, London N2 9PW for *Can it be true* © Allans Publishing (Australia) Pty. Ltd. UK rights administered solely by Stainer & Bell Ltd.

Thankyou Music Ltd, 1 St Anne's Road, Eastbourne, E Sussex BN21 3UN for *Bind us together* © Copyright 1977 Thankyou Music, *Jesus name above all names* © 1974, 1979 Scripture in Song/Thankyou Music, *You shall go out with joy* © Copyright 1975 Lillenas Pub. Co./Thankyou Music, *From heaven you came* © Copyright 1983 Thankyou Music, *Such love* Copyright © Copyright 1982 Thankyou Music, *The King is among us* © Copyright 1981 Thankyou Music, *Be still for the presence of the Lord* © Copyright 1986 Thankyou Music, *O Lord your tenderness* © Copyright 1986 Thankyou Music, *All heaven declares* © Copyright 1987 Thankyou Music, *Hosanna* © Copyright 1985 Mercy Publishing/Thankyou Music, *Lord the light of your love* © Copyright 1987 Make Way Music, and *O let the son of God enfold you* © Copyright 1979 Mercy Publishing/Thankyou Music.

Word Music (UK), a division of Word (UK) Ltd, 9 Holdom Avenue, Bletchley, Milton Keynes, MK1 1QR for *I will enter his gates* © Copyright 1976 Maranatha! Music USA, Father we adore you © Copyright 1972 Maranatha! Music USA, *Open our eyes Lord* © Copyright 1976 Maranatha! Music USA. *I delight greatly in the Lord* © Copyright 1981 Lifestyle Ministries/Word Music (UK), and *In moments like these* © Copyright 1980 C.A. Music USA.

All or some part of the copyright of the following is vested in Kevin Mayhew Ltd, Rattlesden, Bury St Edmunds, Suffolk IP30 0SZ: *Do not be afraid, Peace perfect peace, This world you have made, Lord of my life, If we only seek peace.*

Every effort has been made to trace the owners of copyright material, and we hope that no copyright has been infringed. Pardon is sought and apology is made if the contrary be the case, and a correction will be made in any reprint of this book.